Let Me Take My Sewing Machine

A Collection of Poems

by

Lorna Prudhoe

In memory of Lorna Prudhoe (1930-2015)

a much-loved

wife, mother, mother-in-law,

grandmother, great-grandmother,

sister, sister-in-law, aunt,

friend and neighbour

and a wonderful poet

RIP

'Across the bridge to Paradise lands'

Dedicated

to

Lorna and Ray, Matty, Norma and Steve

Mandy, Kerry, Ian, Dawn and Darren
and all of the great-grandchildren

Sally and Harry

and to
Joanne,
'the light of our lives'
who was 'minded' by her grandma and grandad as a child,
then cared for them at the end of their lives

Contents

Introduction

Lorna Prudhoe (1930-2015) was born Lorna McClennan in the coal-mining town of Washington, which was then in County Durham (it is now Tyne & Wear). With her parents, Matty and Susie McClennan, and her younger sister Sally, she grew up in a close-knit mining community and, despite the war and the hardships of the lives of the miners and their families, she had a happy childhood, surrounded by extended family, friends and neighbours. In 1950 she married Norman Prudhoe and they lived happily together for sixty-five years until her sad death in 2015 at the age of eighty-five.

She loved sewing, cooking, baking, shopping and going to the bingo with her sister (and, until 1983, their mother, Susie). A connoisseur of markets and an extremely sociable woman who knew almost everyone in Washington, the shopping trips she enjoyed so much always took a great deal of time, for she would invariably bump into several people she knew along the way and spend a lot of time chatting, whether she was at Concord (which she always called 'Washington' – '*to call it Concord is a sin*'), the Galleries, South Shields, Chester-le-Street, Sunderland or Newcastle.

Lorna loved her home town, a town which underwent many changes during her lifetime. She liked to remember it as it was during her childhood and youth (*The Flat Tops, Usworth Colliery, Memories On The 294*) and, like many of the town's inhabitants, she was keen to remind people that it was the ancestral home of the first American president, George 'Geordie' Washington (*The Village*). She also extended her gaze beyond Washington itself to include the whole of the north-east and felt an affinity with all Geordies who'd made it in the worlds of entertainment and sport (*North East Talent*).

Her pride in her working-class, Geordie heritage shines through in the many poems she has left us, poems which chronicle her life and the lives of those around her, *real* lives, lived by real people. The world depicted in Lorna's poems is a world where men worked in harsh, constricted conditions underground and subsequently loved the great outdoors; they had allotments, grew their own vegetables and raced pigeons. It is a world where women were proud of their homes and their families, their dresses, their shoes and their hats, whatever their financial circumstances ... and whatever their size! It is a world where children ran free in the wide open spaces, despite the strict rules of family, school and (the catholic) church.

Some of the poems are very funny (*Baking Day, The Mini Bus, Small Outsize*), but many are also tinged with sadness (often, however, lightened by a funny twist at the end – *If Ever*). Some also tackle serious issues. We see glimpses in the poems of Lorna's left-wing political convictions, views inherent in the sort of mining communities she knew so well. She always loved listening to the speeches at the annual Durham Miners' Gala (*Durham Big Meeting*) and her favourite politician (and mine) was Tony Benn, who always supported the miners. Her pacifism, born out of a desire for everyone to get on, is also apparent in the more serious *Bush's War*.

To me she was Auntie Lorna, one of the most important people in my life. I share her interest in our cultural heritage and our own family's history, her socialist politics, her pacifism and her passion for writing. My novels and her poems might be very different, but they spring from the same roots and she was thrilled when I chose the name McClennan (her maiden name and, of course, my mother's) for my fictional detective.

Many of the poems in this collection were written to mark happy family occasions - weddings, anniversaries and other celebrations - but Lorna could also find inspiration in the most normal, everyday activities, such as baking, sewing, simply seeing something out of her window, or bumping into someone at the shops. It has also struck me, on re-reading all of the poems, how often she felt inspired whilst travelling on buses. I can identify with this, for I have sat many a time on the X1 to Newcastle or the Fab56, mentally working out plots and composing scenes for my latest novel. *2022* even begins with the heroine sitting on a bus, gazing out of the window, before something dramatic happens. Lorna would also gaze out of bus windows and she would reminisce about the places the bus passed, not as she could see them that day, but as they had been during her childhood (*Memories On The 294*). Even meeting people she didn't know while travelling from one place to another (*Stranger On The Bus*) could inspire her to write.

Her writing, like her sewing and her cooking, reminds us that creativity does not belong solely to the middle classes, but thrives in our northern working-class communities. She did not have the benefit of a higher education, but she had a real talent for writing, a way with words which was warm, amusing and very clever. She liked a twist – *Going For Gold,* for example, is apparently a poem about Great Britain's staging of the Olympic Games in 2012, but turns out to be an homage to her beloved husband, who was never an athlete, but worked down the pit for forty-three years. Norman's presence can, in fact, be detected in almost all of the poems. He is 'Prudhoe', he is 'the pigeon fancier', he is 'my man'.

Family and friends meant everything to Lorna and many of the poems reflect this. In later years she wrote about her children, her grandchildren, her sister, her niece and nephews and many others from her 'present', whilst also reflecting on those important to her in the past – her own parents (*Mother, Dad's Allotment*) and grandparents (*Granda, Between Rivers*), her aunts and uncles (*Aunt Sally*), her cousin (*My Cousin Alice*).

Auntie Lorna passed away in September 2015. Appropriately, Jimmy Nail's *Big River* was played at her funeral. Perhaps her most literary poem, the beautiful *Someday,* was read by her granddaughter Mandy and *If Ever* was printed in the Order of Service.

Uncle Norman died only five months later, aged 89.

Re-reading the poems reminded us all of how good they are and, feeling that others may like to share them, we put together this collection and published them, first as an e-book, and now as a paperback.

Incidentally, if you are wondering about the title of this book, you need to read the very last poem to 'get it'. She loved her sewing machine!

Alison Greaves
December 2015, revised February 2017

Memories On The 294

I love to ride on the 294,
Past places where I've been before,
Through Glebe Village to the shops,
Where long queues are waiting at the stops.

Past Albany where the long road bends,
Always known as the Pit Road Ends.
We reach Washington and the New Inn,
To call it Concord is a sin.

Up the Drive to Wellbank Road,
Passing by my old abode.
Great stone dwellings now adorn
The humble place where I was born.

Vivid memories now take over,
Fields of buttercups, milkmaids' clover.
Oats and barley, grass and wheat
Ripening gold in the summer heat.

Working farmyards can be seen,
The tithe barn standing near the Green,
Lovely walks along the Leam,
Picking blackberries by the stream.

The bomb crater at Whittle Burn,
Childhood memories still return.
Down the Coach Road to Usworth Comp,
Where Flat Top children used to romp.

Watching for dad coming home,
Covered in coal dust, on his own.
The tuneful whistle was his alone,
After a long shift, never a moan.

To Waterloo, through the hole in the wall,
Three streets nestling by Usworth Hall.
Aunt Anne and grandma waiting there,
Sitting on their horsehair chair.

Home-made pies they always baked,
Pans of broth and stottie cakes.
No colliery child could ask for more.
Nostalgia on the 294.

Between Rivers

The earliest sound I ever heard
Was the endearing lilt of the Geordie word.
Everyone knew this mam of mine,
Spent her childhood by the Tyne.

Grandma with her gleaming pinny,
Her 'bonny lass' and her 'howay hinny!'
She sang 'Up Come Paddy' for Sally and me,
Bouncing the bairns upon her knee.

Newcastle, electric atmosphere,
And Geordie people I love to hear.
Reminds me of when I was a child,
Having fun and running wild.

Now riding the metro on the lines,
Counting the bridges of the Tyne,
The beautiful buildings of Grainger Street,
The Green Market, a flowering treat.

As I grow older, the sounds I hear,
Are the familiar accents of the Wear.

Coal Miners

Close together in the cage,
About to earn their hard-earned wage,
Side by side, like brother to brother,
Watching out for each other.

Four miles under the great North Sea,
Pneumoconiosis and shattered knee.
Most miners know their share of pain.
You won't see their likes again.

Think of football or pigeon race,
While cutting coal along the face.
Up above the sky is bright,
Down below eternal night.

Now miners are a dying breed.
For the coal there is no need.
Still they use the open-cast,
While the countryside they blast.

The pit-head wheels, they have all gone.
The dole queues now are very long.
Men play football on the site.
Now it is the Stadium of Light.

Dad's Allotment

I often think about our dad.
I think of all the fun we had.
He had an allotment by the stream,
Or was this just a childhood dream?

Every day he would go there,
Whenever he had time to spare.
Where has all that water gone?
The tributary to the River Don.

Dad was tall and had white hair.
Mam and dad were always there.
Lots of love, with time to play,
In those idyllic summer days.

Dad won prizes for his beet,
Tasty, tender and very sweet.
Dark red carnations he grew with pride,
Around the paths and side by side.

I remember to this very day,
He gave half his veg away.
No-one seemed to crave for more
In those far off days before the war.

Childhood At The Flat Tops

Oh, for the fun of yesterday,
When all children went out to play!
No television or computers.
We all played marbles in the gutters.

Spinning tops and skipping ropes,
Double Dutch if you could cope.
Stotting balls off someone's wall,
Getting wrong off Mrs Hall.

Chalking hopscotch on the path,
Shouting 'You're out!' What a laugh!
Joe Shaw's Lonnen, Topper Swinburne's meadows,
Clapping the boys practising headers.

Waterloo fields and the Old Coach Road.
To be nice to old people was a strict code.
Cotton dresses were the rule.
You wore gym frocks to go to school.

No leisure trainers in the past,
You had to make your sandshoes last.
If I could put back the sands of time
When all I was, was eight or nine.

Jumping dickers on the burn,
The boys went in with nothing on.
Getting to Mass was no fuss,
Everyone piled on the Waterloo bus.

Milly Dingle had a wooden shop
Sinclairs' store was at the top.
Tomato paste, home-made bread and jam,
I was sent to Milly's for American spam.

We ate fish and chips, I've no doubt,
To help the war-time rations out.
Went to the pictures whenever we could,
To see a film from Hollywood.

Shirley Temple, Bette Davis, Errol Flynn
Took us to a world we'd never seen.
Laurel and Hardy made us laugh.
We saw them all at the Ritz or the Gaffe.

Everyone seemed very pally.
We loved our grandparents and Aunt Sally.
Dad's garden wasn't far to go,
Between High Row and Quarry Row.
We spent hours there happily
Helping dad dig for victory.

When dad's turn came for Pensher View
I thought my heart would break in two.
My childhood ended on that day,
But Flat Top memories will always stay.

Usworth Colliery

I often think about the past,
All the years have gone so fast;
The kindly neighbours, all close-knit,
In the streets around the pit.

The colliery green, piled high with logs,
The pit pond that was full of frogs,
The wooden mangle, the big coal pail,
The tin bath hanging from a nail.

The sound of hobnails on the path,
Before they built the pithead baths;
Just yesterday, or so it seems,
Dad mending belts on Usworth screens.

The oven with its round iron door,
From the ceiling to the floor;
On the cracket with the cat,
My mother's home-made proggy mat.

Edith Avenue's two long streets,
With every doorway nice and neat;
The miners' park, the brickworks too,
Near the road to Waterloo.

The old Dole school, quite near the houses,
Where the girls made Pawson's blouses;
The coal trucks rumbling on the lines,
Back and forward to the Tyne.

On Hunter's bus we rode with pride,
From Waterloo to Waterside.
The countryside and all its joys,
The miners and the Bevin Boys.

I pass the colliery now and again,
Without the pit, it's not the same.

The Village

The very centre of our town,
In my mind 'the jewel in the crown',
It was there in ancient times,
Long before they sank the mines.

The village now is dressed in green,
Loveliest place I've ever seen.
First to church and then to school,
Where I was taught to follow rules.

St. Joseph's, where I was often late,
Mr. Battle waiting by the gate.
Lambeth's, Plender's and Winder's shop,
If we had a penny, in we'd pop.

Mr. Riley's songs I won't forget.
His beautiful music is with me yet.
Miss Fitzsimmons' needlework I adore.
They taught us all right through the war.

The old Cross Keys and Washington Arms,
The library that had many charms,
The Rectory and the Bobby Lees,
The orchards and the apple trees.

The old men's hut and horses' trough,
The little park is not there now.
Shoeing horses could be seen,
May processions around the green.

At Kear's fish shop we were queueing,
When the Old Hall was a ruin.
Tina Sweeney in the farmers' club,
Made us cocoa in a very big jug.

Before the Washingtons crossed the sea,
Where George chopped down the cherry tree,
The Old Hall's there for all to see,
It has a place in history.

Beattie Bunny's

There was once a shop in Washington,
I think you'd like to know;
Quite near the New Inn corner
Some eighty years ago.

The name which stood above the door
I thought was very funny.
The little lady who owned the shop –
Her name was Beattie Bunny!

She sold haberdashery and bric-a-brac,
Wool of every type and shade,
Bobbins of thread and fountain pens,
Matches and razor blades.

If ever you went shopping,
To Jones's or the Store,
You always went to Beattie's.
No-one could sell you more!

Cards of pins and needles
Were hung up on the wall.
She had a little ladder,
As she really was quite small!

I remember the streets of Washington
From when I too was small,
But Bettie Bunny's little shop
Was my favourite of them all.

Granda

He lived in Jarrow as a lad.
His mother died, he left his dad.
A boy soldier he became.
Harry Jennings was his name.

Told us tales about the wars.
In Africa he fought the Boers.
Ypres, Passchendaele and the Mons,
Awful Gallipoli and the Somme.

In India he served with the Raj.
He could have lived there, free of charge.
In the Durhams he was proud.
He stood out in any crowd.

In between he worked the mines,
Quite a few from Wear to Tyne.
A rosy face and Jerry crop,
His bowler hat perched on the top.

A Sergeant Major in his prime,
A well-known character of his time.
Every Sunday off to Mass.
Very few pubs he would pass.

Everything in moderation, he'd say,
As in the back door he would sway.
A white stiff collar and blackened boots,
A straight-back soldier to the roots.

Two soldiers came in '39,
They took our granda from the mine.
He was too old to go to war,
But he trained young soldiers as before.

He loved us in his very own way,
But he found it hard to say.

Mother

If I could pick and not be choosy,
I couldn't pick a better mam than Susie.
She listened to all our fears and tears,
Always had a sympathetic ear.

She didn't smoke and hated curses,
But she loved a bet upon the horses.
Right to the end she wore her hats.
She was well-known along the Flats.

A very good cook, she was no sloven,
Baked cakes and pies in the big coal oven.
Dad worked long hours and did his best,
To see Sally and me were both well-dressed.

She was widowed in nineteen-sixty-one,
We tried to see she was never alone.
She loved the town and the theatre,
And a day at the races really pleased her.

Her grandchildren were her pride and joy,
Three lovely girls and three handsome boys.
I hope from Heaven she can tell,
That they are all doing really well.

When people saw us they would quip,
'Here comes Susie and her chicks!'

Aunt Sally

A girl in the twenties was our aunt Sal,
Like an older sister and a very good pal.
Her sweet face we'll never forget;
The gentle voice is with us yet.

Refined, her principles were strong.
She put us right when we were wrong.
Her tailored clothes were always neat,
Crocodile court shoes on her feet.

Madam Pallister permed her hair,
A marcel wave to make you stare.
A lovely cup she won long ago,
For doing the Charleston with a garter that showed.

Her faith meant everything to her.
I know in Heaven she's in God's care.
As I get older she's with me more.
She's only waiting on a far off shore.

My Cousin Alice

From the Felling, here they come!
Alice Montgomery and her mum.

We make a noise in grandma's flat.
Granda isn't pleased about that.

We then dress up in auntie's firs,
The dark one mine, the light one hers.

Giggle and laugh at grandma's hat,
I get my ears boxed for that.

Ran wild on Waterloo fields; got dirty,
Oh, what fun we had in the thirties!

Usworth pit heap was a plateau high,
Table Mountain in my mind's eye.

Took little Sally to Usworth Park,
The Lizzies and the tea-pot lid were a lark.

It's not the same now, the joy has gone.
I'll ring her now before too long.

Her health is poor, she's had her pain,
But my cousin Alice is just the same.

We'll Meet Again

I can't remember a nicer day.
To the Customs House we're on our way.
On a trip with the happy crowd,
Singing war-time songs out loud.

War-time memories will never die,
The spitfire in the starry sky,
The union jacks a-flying high,
The servicemen all marching by.

The airman who was dressed in blue,
The soldier and the sailor too.
The blackout warden and the sirens wailed.
To jerk the heart, it never failed.

The cheeky chappie and Noel Coward,
Eric Morecambe and Frankie Howerd,
Judy Garland and Gracie Fields' songs,
You just had to sing along.

'The Yanks are coming!' and 'In the mood',
The jitterbugging was oh so good.
Ivor Novello's dancing years.
Brought me very close to tears.

Homeward bound without a care,
With bittersweet memories of yesteryear.

Schooldays

I wish I'd worked hard when at school.
Why did I have to act the fool?
Why didn't I use the brains I had
To make my parents very glad?

Behind a wall to have a smoke,
Thinking what a funny joke!
We didn't believe the old wives' tales
That Wild Woodbines were coffin nails.

At fourteen I worked for the Co-op Store,
Making men's suits by the score.
From eight to six I served my time
In the CWS factory, Pelaw-on-Tyne.

I've cleaned and cooked in factories and schools,
And I've stuck closely to the rules.
I've learned many skills along the way,
I use them till this very day.

My three children were of higher grade.
They didn't make the mistakes I made.
They all worked hard and made me proud.
I'd like to praise them very loud.

If I could live my life again,
I would most likely do the same.
I'd still stick closely to the rules,
But I'd work harder when at school.

All Our Yesterdays

Last night I went right back in time,
To stitching jackets on the line,
Working with the Geordie girls.
Everyone had corkscrew curls.

The music playing in the past
Made us do our sewing fast.
The lovely words of 'Once In A While';
A secret memory makes me smile.

'The Dream of Olwyn' and 'Clair de Lune'
'Some Other Time' and 'Elmer's Tune'.
American swing, jitterbug and jive,
Made us all feel so alive.

The wondrous beat of 'The Sabre Dance'.
We'd dance on the belt if given the chance!
Joseph Locke and his 'Last Goodbye',
The sad melody of 'As Time Goes By'.

By half past five I'm home again
Hurrying down our colliery lane.
A meal, a wash and make-up on,
Catch Hunter's bus to Washington.

Saturday Dances At The Miners' Welfare Hall

We all looked forward to Saturday night,
All dressed up and feeling right.
On that springy floor we would prance,
Even the girls who couldn't dance.

Make-up on and hair in curls,
Quickstep and foxtrot, doing our twirls.
Twelve Street Rag and Tiger Bay,
Jitterbugging in our very own way.

Danny McCourt's band had a great beat.
He had us all up on our feet.
The hokey-cokey and ball-in-the-jack,
Sometimes the conga, just for a laugh.

The evening passed as fast as could be,
For Joanie, Rhoda, Marian and me.
The pubs closed then at ten at night,
Then in came the lads, most of them tight.

We gave those lads a certain glance,
Wishing they'd ask us up to dance.
But someone's trying to ruin our night.
Very often it ends in a fight!

My Man

In our garden, there he stands,
Tin of pigeon corn in his hands.
Every now and then it rattles.
They pick about like a herd of cattle.

'Get in the loft, pet,' I hear him say,
'Your dinner's ready', I always pray.
I don't mind, I feel his joy,
He's had his pigeons since he was a boy.

The first time I met him, he was tight.
I thought at the time he wasn't right,
But we liked each other straight away.
Thank heavens for that lucky day!

That such a man could fancy me!
To me he's always twenty-three.

Down the mine for forty-three years.
When he left there were no tears.
He never asked that much from life,
Just his family and his wife.

Prudhoe

He came from Northumberland, so the story goes,
A very young man, his name Prudhoe.

To help to sink the Washington shafts,
Chain and nail-making was his craft.

He loved this town and multiplied,
All of his family by his side.

Quite a lot, as you will know,
Carry the title of Prudhoe.

The Northumberland Percys are his kin,
How it happened, I can't begin.

I wonder why this man of mine
Spent a lifetime down the mine.

Oxclose Dene

We loved to go to Oxclose Dene,
The prettiest place you've ever seen.
The babbling stream and broken tree,
Bluebells as far as you could see.

We picnicked by the old mine shaft
While the children ran and laughed,
Past Hankie's Farm to Shedden's Hill
Mental pictures are with me still.

The fir trees now are very tall,
Planted when my bairns were small.
Over the stream fields they would skip,
Followed closely by our Gyp.

Returning via the old Cook's Hall,
Badgers and rabbits, as I recall.
The rope is gone now from the tree
Where Matty would climb so happily.

Three horses gambling in the grass
Come towards us as we pass,
Through Doctor Kidd's and over the stiles,
Buttercups and daisies for miles and miles.

An adventure park where children play.
You knew that they were safe all day.

The bulldozers came with their awful sound,
They put the stream beneath the ground.
The Oxclose Dene we all adore
Now somewhere under the Galleries' floor.

Durham Big Meeting

It's mid-July and we're on our way.
Today is the Miners' Gala day.
Down the road with great elation,
On the way to Usworth Station.
With the band in the Guards' Van,
Packed like sardines in a can.

With arms entwined, we sway from side to side,
Following our colliery banner with pride.
Stop for a rest at the market place,
Bobbies stand around, just in case.

Count the dignitaries on the balcony.
There's Tony Benn, waving down at me!
The Silver Band pauses at the County Hotel,
Playing the miners' hymns we know so well.

Nearly at the race-course, weary as can be,
Longing for our sandwiches and a nice cup of tea.
The music of the fairground gives a festive sound,
And hundreds of banners are all around the ground.

The Tories broke our union. It was a mortal sin.
They said that our brave miners were the enemy within.

In the centre is a platform full of noble men,
Giving fervent speeches of injustice done to them.
Some day I won't be going, as I fall fast asleep,
But I know that my soul will march down Silver Street.

The Mini Bus

'I think I'll sit one seat behind,'
Said husband, trying to be kind.
'Keep tight a hold, or you'll fall out
When going round the roundabout'.

Alighting passengers hide a smile
At my legs stretched out in the aisle.
Thankfully, it's short runs on the bus.
It wasn't made for the likes of us.

Back and forwards to the shops,
All day long, it never stops.
Past Biddick, down to Brady Square,
Pick up passengers waiting there.

Through the Village, there's no dispute,
It really is the scenic route.
Through Oxclose and Blackfell to Dickens' store,
The Garden Centre we adore.

Past the décor and the modern art,
If I had money we soon would part!
Home improvements we discuss,
Then back home on the mini bus.

Friday

On the ten-to-ten bus to Chester-le-Street.
It takes me on my special treat,
Right down classy Biddick Lane,
Now that summer's here again.

Through Harraton, Rickleton and Old Picktree,
St. George's Estate among the trees,
Shrubs and bushes of every shade of green,
Flowers on verges meant to be seen.

Lumley Castle in all its glory,
Great stone walls, old in story.
Browse among stalls all on my own.
Chat to traders, I'm not alone.

Stalls laid out for all to see.
They put on a show, just for me.
Back to the Gala for tea and a scone,
A game of bingo, then head for home.

My Sewing Machine

The greatest treasure that I own
Is resting on its wooden throne.
Almost every day it's used,
Old, battered and abused.
I never craved for any other,
My 1960s 'Jones Brother'.

The over-locker works like a dream,
To finish off my half-inch seam.
I think I'll make a dress for Lorna,
Or will it be a top for Norma?

I love to hear the motor zoom
In my little sewing room.
A great challenge, you will know,
To make size 12 into 24.

Remnants all around the floor,
Black bin liners out the door.
The sweetest thing I've ever seen,
My lovely little sewing machine.

Small Outsize

I really would love to be slim,
Not bulging all over, but trim.
I'd dress in the latest of elegance,
Step out with the greatest of confidence.
Oh yes, I'd love to be slim!

Been a failure at each slimming club,
The trouble is, I love my grub!
Mr Blobby has nothing on me.
I eat far too much for my tea.
Oh yes, I would love to be slim!

People would value me much more
If I didn't take size twenty-four!
Oh yes, I would love to be slim!

My shoes would be the latest style,
No more flat ones all the while.
My clothes from Fenwicks I'd treasure,
Copy the styles with my famous tape measure.
Oh yes, I would love to be slim!

I think I'll have one more go.
I really am walking too slow.
Oh, to jump on a bus
With the minimum of fuss!
Oh yes, I would love to be slim!

Me

It must have happened overnight.
I think I look an awful sight!
They say the mirror never lies,
One more wrinkle around the eyes.

I cannot even reach my zip.
I know I look a proper clip!
When did this change come about?
Age is cruel, there's no doubt.

I'll ask Judith to perm my hair,
Get some brand new clothes to wear,
Then do something about my feet,
A pair of Clark's springers, what a treat!

With shoulders back and head held high,
Face the crowd, I won't be shy.
Enjoy bingo and love a bet,
What you see is what you get.

Penshaw Monument

A majestic edifice way up high,
The Temple of Diana in my mind's eye,
All by itself, it's standing still,
Lord Lambton's monument on Penshaw Hill.

It overlooks the lovely Wear,
Of folklore and legend we hold dear.
Griddle Cake Cottage and the Lambton Worm,
It ate cattle and bairns and made you squirm.
Of the Earl of Perth and his strange life,
He took a local lass for his wife.

Coal mines and shipyards all long gone,
But still the river flows along.
I open the curtains to greet the morn.
There it stands in the early dawn.

No matter how far away you roam,
When you see it in the distance, you're almost home.

The Pigeon Fancier

With trained eye, he scans the sky,
Watching whilst his pigeons fly.
Sitting there, he never tires,
Hoping they don't hit the wires.

Ian takes them for a chuck,
I hope that this will change his luck.
Oh, Sundays really make me laugh!
That's the day they have their bath.

Words of love, like 'Howay, lass!'
As they alight upon the grass.
Around his feet the young birds linger,
To peck the titbit from his finger.

The tin is rattled, they drop with speed.
It's time to see the pigeons feed.
Content and happy you can see
On his arm and on his knee.

Endearing words I've never heard
Are whispered to his special bird.
To keep them well he really tries,
So he gazes in their eyes.

They circle high with angels' grace,
I'd love to see him win a race.

North East Talent

I'm so lazy, it must be said.
All day long I've sat and read
About a Geordie called Jimmy Nail,
A heart-warming, fascinating tale.

Tim Healy, James Bolam and Robson Green,
Often on the telly screen.
Brian Ferry in the charts,
Alan Price and his Jarrow March.

Rowan Atkinson's Mr Bean,
The funniest man I've ever seen.
Kevin Whateley is there, of course,
Loved him in Inspector Morse.

Denise Welch, Sting and Jimmy Nail,
The lovely Geordie in Emmerdale,
Alan Shearer, Gazza's limbs,
Frank Wappat and his songs and hymns.

Jill Halfpenny's skills made her a star,
Always knew she would go far.
To all that talent, my hands I clap
They put the north-east on the map.

Added by Tony, Lorna's nephew:
Auntie Lorna, bloomin' heck!
How could you forget about Ant and Dec?

Baking Day

I think I'll bake a batch of scones,
Making sure the oven's turned on.

Corned beef, onion and potato pies.
I only hope my cake will rise.

A cheese and onion, and sausage rolls,
Mixing more pastry in the bowl.

A rhubarb pie will do the trick,
And so six sticks I quickly pick.

Macaroons and sweet mince pies,
A spread for anybody's eyes.

Cooling nicely on the trays.
How I enjoy my baking days!

Norman shouts: 'Don't make any more!
The stuff is coming out the door!'

I hope that someone comes for tea,
There's far too much for him and me.

Where to put it is a teaser.
Bung the whole lot in the freezer!

Shopping Day

I think I'll do a bit of shopping,
So to the Galleries I'll be popping.

The mini-link stops at the top,
Then a little look around the In Shops.

Put a coin in the shopping trolley.
I'm on my way, it's quite jolly.

Now should I go to Savacentre?
Into the big doors I will enter.

Have a glance at the textiles,
Then make my way to other aisles.

Make a note of what is spent,
Don't forget about the rent!

Chat to friends, that's always nice,
Then complain about the price.

By now my legs have turned to jelly,
There's our Sally on the deli!

Fifteen years serving bacon and cheese,
She has always tried to please.

By now I'm almost fit to drop,
Into the taxi I soon will pop.

Sally

Sally and I have always been mates.
We meet every Monday, I can hardly wait.
Browse around Joplings, they know what to charge,
But we're just as happy in Bon Marche.

Jackie Whites and the Bridges next,
Then on to West Street for the rest,
Down to Holmside and, oh, by jingo!
Into the Top Rank for a game of bingo.

On special nights out, she will impress.
Since she was little she's loved her dress.
Always knows just what's in fashion,
Studies accessories with great passion.

She and Harry love their holidays,
She's had a job since her schooldays.
She loves her family like no other,
Is a lovely sister, wife and mother.

By this rhyme, I think you will see
My little sister Sally is a big part of me.

Christmas Shopping

Christmas shopping in the town,
Gives you a lift when you feel down.
Buskers all along the street,
The atmosphere is quite unique.

Marks & Spencer's, Barrett's shoes,
Which is first? Which will I choose?
Beautiful textiles, I'm spoiled for choice.
'Careful', says my inner voice.

To W.H. Smith I then will pop,
Buy DVDs from the music shop.
I'll buy a cornet and have a rest.
To save my legs, I'll do my best.

The crowd around Fenwick's is now three deep.
When they move on I'll take a peep.
Gulliver turned and our eyes met.
I swear that is the best one yet.

Past Brunswick Church to Monument Mall,
The Newcastle United shop I recall.
Black and white stripes are the Geordies' pride,
But a soft spot for Sunderland I can't hide.

On the metro to the terminus,
Then at Heworth I catch my bus.
In twenty minutes I'll be there,
Step down like a lady at Brady Square.

Saturday With Ena

Saturday morning is here again,
The weatherman says it will not rain.
Check to see I've got plenty of money,
To be stuck without it wouldn't be funny.

Where to today? There's no hassle,
South Shields, Sunderland or Newcastle.
'Where do you fancy?' I always say;
When Ena's ready, we're on our way.

The shopping we do is not a lot,
Odds and ends, bits and bobs we forgot.
Newcastle is a lovely city,
Elegant people all look pretty.

Northumberland Street, Eldon Square and Grainger,
We know the whole town, we're no strangers.
In Sunderland we feel at home,
At South Shields market we love to roam.

In summer we go further afield,
Whitley Bay, Tynemouth and sometimes North Shields.
After a cup of tea and a scone,
We jump on the metro and head for home.

Sally's Leaving Do

It's our Sally's leaving do tonight.
We're all dressed up and looking bright.
Norman's wearing his Marksy's shirt,
I have a new blouse and pleated skirt.
The Football Club? How do we get there?
It's right next door to Washington Welfare!

There's Sally, Anne and the two Harrys,
Ella, Alison and the two Garrys,
Julie, Jayne and Tony, he never changes;
Loves to walk on mountain ranges.

The disco starts, it's quite loud.
The deli girls are a jolly crowd.
We all queue up for the food.
The long table's groaning, this is good.
The speeches are over, it's all okay,
Sally is presented with a huge bouquet.

As the night wears on we all get merry.
Sally will miss her friends at the deli.
I pray to God we all will stay
Content and happy as we are today.
And I hope I get a taste of that cake
That Susan took such pains to make!

Lorna

In comes Lorna for a natter,
Makes us laugh with her jolly chatter.
She has an IQ second to none,
I had her when I was twenty-one.

Head of House at Usworth School,
To be a good teacher was her golden rule.
A weekend in London to see a show,
To wear a new outfit, off they go!

Then off to somewhere posh for their tea,
And Fortnum & Mason for a present for me.
She loves Blackpool in September,
With Madge and her mates it's a time to remember.

The rest of her time is for the comp.
It's built on the fields where I used to romp.

Matty

Matty is my only lad,
The living image of my dad.
When he pops in I jump for joy.
The girls call him my blue-eyed boy.

Every weekend he goes fishing,
To catch a big one he is wishing.
But, never mind, he's had his woe,
He lost his friend Les not long ago.

Margaret was also very ill.
Cured now, thank Heavens, she's with us still.
I hope his worries are now all over.
Win the lottery and be in clover!

To look after his family he's very reliant,
A nurse once called him a gentle giant.
A lovely family – he has five,
Must be the proudest man alive.

They all have brains and all are beauties,
The twins are both his little cuties!

Norma

She walks past the window and I can tell,
Aloof and tall, like a young gazelle,
Pops her head around the door.
'It's only me!' Who could ask for more?

Her cheery face lights up the room.
Her personality shifts the gloom.
Tells us all about her day.
Make her happy, I always pray.

Being independent, she always planned,
On her own two feet she firmly stands.
Her lovely flat is quite a treat,
Plants and ornaments, very neat.

The decorating she did on her own,
With ideas taken from House & Home.
The bathroom has just been installed
With plastered ceilings and new walls.

My Grandchildren

Six young people with social graces,
Down to earth and beautiful faces,
All grown up and very bright,
Happiness is their God-given right.

Dawn and Darren are the twins,
Enquiring minds and cheeky grins.
Mandy, Ian and Kerry have their own spaces,
All with jobs and going places.

Joanne lets you know she's there,
Bright of eye and dark curly hair.
Affection that I can't explain,
When they get hurt I feel the pain.

Make them happy all through life,
Free from trouble, free from strife.
If you think I'm boasting, as well you might,
I'm their grandma and I have the right!

Joanne

The light of our lives is our Joanne.
She comes to see us whenever she can.
Tells us jokes around the houses,
Wears tight jeans and sloppy blouses.

Sometimes so laid back she's horizontal,
Next time vexed, she's nearly mental.
She has her dinner with us every Sunday,
And often drops in on a Thursday.

A keen fan of Newcastle United,
When they are playing she gets excited.
She's seventeen and quite a cutey.
I know some day she'll be a beauty.

She's gobby and we know she's there,
Rosy face and dark curly hair,
A gleam in her eye and quite stroppy,
Never seen without her pet dog Poppy.

She adores her mam and dad,
The only one they ever had.

Sally And Harry's Ruby Wedding

The Stella Maris is packed tonight,
Coloured lights are flashing bright.
Music coming from the stage,
Disco dancing all the rage.

Buffet food across the hall,
Stretching from wall to wall.
Every taste your heart could wish
For, beautiful food in every dish.

The reason for this great elation,
A ruby wedding celebration.
Congratulations at the door,
Alex jiving on the floor.

Friends and relations from near and far
Come by taxi; left the car.
So Sally and Harry, we all say,
Congratulations on your special day.

May you both have many more,
As nice as the years that have gone before.
Your lovely family have done you proud,
A happy, contented, united crowd.

Edinburgh

I really can't believe my eyes.
This is such a nice surprise.
On the train, it's Lorna's treat,
My two daughters, oh, so sweet.

Queueing with the happy crowds
To see the castle in the clouds.
We take a look into old St. Giles,
Pilgrims kneeling in the aisles.

Clan crests of every gilt,
Celtic crosses and swinging kilt.
The lone piper plays very loud,
Welcoming the visiting crowd.

The Scottish blood flows very strong,
Where our ancestors all belong.
You know that you've been here before
With your ain folk in days of yore.

We take a stroll down Princes Street,
Shop around for a bite to eat.
An Italian deli down the road,
They end up with a heavy load.

Visit the department stores,
Ride the lifts from floor to floor.
Find the perfume my girls adore.
Well stocked, they can carry no more.

To Waverley Station for the train,
Some day we'll all come back again
On a lovely sunny day.
It's just an hour and a half away.

Tony And Jayne's Wedding

This is the wedding of the year.
A people carrier got us here.
Glorious sunshine all the way
For Jayne and Tony's special day.

A silver castle on the hill,
Half a dozen miles from Rhyl.
New-born lambs and an ancient tree,
A lovely view of the Irish Sea.

The wedding's held at the Church of Wales.
That old church could tell some tales.
Here comes Jayne on her father's arm,
A picture of happiness and charm.

The ladies dressed in elegant hats,
The men in tailcoats and cravats.
Lauren with her happy smile,
Everyone is dressed in style.

The Kinmel Manor with its lovely grounds,
Beautiful country all around.
Neale and Alex enjoy their stay,
In the swimming pool every day.

The feast is served in the banqueting hall,
An enjoyable time for one and all.
Disco dancing and cheek to cheek,
Showaddywaddy, then Zorba the Greek.

Sunday and it's time to leave,
Many thanks to our special Jeeves.
A lovely lunch from Bronwyn and Clive,
Hope we all get home by five.

Bush's War

This bloodshed I just can't abide.
It makes me want to run and hide.
Innocent people with shattered parts,
Screaming women with broken hearts.

Those weapons that were never found
And never hidden underground,
This awful war that Bush had planned
That made him want to bomb their land.

Now the devil is abroad,
We've helped unleash the evil hordes.
Young soldiers risking all their lives,
Leaving children and young wives.

Please make it all come to an end.
No more young men will we send,
No more foreign lands will we spoil
To get our hands upon their oil.

The Yanks and us must share the blame,
We all should hang our heads in shame.
Those people of a different creed,
To bomb their land there was no need.

Springtime

I'm watching for the signs of spring
And all the pleasures it will bring.
Golden daffodils peeping through,
Hyacinths yellow, mauve and blue.

No more frost in the early morn,
The drone of mowers on the lawn,
The sound of starlings and the ring-neck dove,
Cotton wool clouds up above.

Goodbye to food served piping hot,
Basins of broth and tatie pot,
Mince and dumplings and yorkshire pud,
All that stodge that tastes so good.

For years I've longed for a patio.
Maybe this year, you never know.
A flower garden like a dream,
Even the coal bunkers painted green.

Now shall we go to Spain or Rome?
Or, just like last year, stay at home?
Looking forward to things that please
And Norman walking with new knees!

A Day At The Coast

This lovely day belongs to me,
Paddling in the great North Sea.

South Shields, Sunderland, it doesn't matter,
As long as I hear that Geordie chatter.

I'll try not to go too far in.
I never did learn how to swim.

The sun is shining, it's quite nice,
But the blooming sea is cold as ice!

Enjoyed fish and chips in the park,
Feeling like a basking shark.

Chips should never pass my lips,
They do nothing for my hips.

I'll walk it off along the shore,
Determined not to eat any more.

Off to Tynemouth Antiques Fair,
20p on the metro will get me there.

Some nice stuff without a doubt,
Others, I've chucked better out!

Pots and pans and carnival glass,
Things mother used when she was a lass.

Nostalgia takes over, I hide the tears,
For a happy life in bygone years.

I then remember how lucky I am,
For my brilliant family and my lovely man.

Stranger On The Bus

I met a lady the other day,
Very tiny, old and grey.
She waved and gave the seat a pat.
All she wanted was a chat.

She'd been a widow for forty-four years,
Seen lots of hardship, worry and cares.
Lost her husband underground,
Her lovely family scattered around.

That day was my anniversary.
What happened to her could have happened to me.
I realised how blessed I've been,
Fifty-five years tret like a queen.

She got off the bus at the shops.
I stayed on for a couple of stops.
I hope some day I'll meet again,
That lovely lady from Easington Lane.

The Stadium

While travelling home on the Fab56,
I'd been to hospital to have my fix,
I then discovered a wonderful sight,
Sunderland fans, in red and white.

The sun looked down on this splendid day,
The morning mist had been swept away.
There were lots of happy girls and boys,
With smiling faces, full of the joys.

Tall and short, large and thin,
They hoped to see the Black Cats win.
Making their way through the narrow lanes,
Topping the league would be their aim.

The Colliery Inn had its doors open wide,
Crowds of people on the paths outside.
The bus slowed down just near the site
Where supporters queued at the Stadium of Light.

The wonderful sight gave me so much pleasure,
The memory I shall keep for ever.
The Davey lamp tells us that a long time ago
There was once a coal mine down below.

The Diamond Wedding

It's sixty years since we've been wed
And this is what my granda said:

'Many a ship has run aground
For want of tar and timber,
Many a love has fallen apart
For want of sticking together.
Never, ever part on a row,
Always make it up somehow.'

'Most men will never give a toss
If you let them think that they're the boss.
Coal miners should always be well fed.'
That is what my mother said.
'Be kind and loving to each other,
And *never* run back to your mother!'

You'll realise I've been no fool,
Sticking close to all these rules.
I thank heaven for my happy life.
I think I've been a loving wife!

Start Walking

Today I walked right down our street.
Did fresh air ever smell so sweet?
The grass verges were so very green.
Today I carried out my dream!

It's two years now since I've been out.
I'm so happy, I want to shout.
I walked right down to Archie's shop,
Never once allowing myself to stop.

And now my heart is full of hope.
I love the visit of the pope.
If you have faith, if you have not,
Please make the most of what you've got.

While feeling safe in my arm-chair,
Self-pity never gets me there.
It's time I got up on my feet,
And start by walking down our street!

Getting Better

I've not been very far this year.
Durham Big Meeting or the Hoppings fair.
I never saw the Red Arrows fly
Or the Tall Ships sailing by.

Sitting here like two old crocks,
Watching it happen on the box,
I long to be out there, in a crowd,
Following the banners and singing loud.

I think it's time I faced the truth.
I'm no longer in my youth.
The bus stops now seem further still.
It's just like climbing up a hill.

I use a lot of taxi cabs.
I'm getting friendly with the lads.
They ferry me where I want to go.
Before they're told, they seem to know.

I tell myself that I'm not ill.
I'll rub my joints and take my pill.
Next year I'll be with all the rest.
To enjoy my life I'll do my best.

Going For Gold

I've watched the Olympics all week long;
Those athletes are so young and strong.
The pole vault, sprint and javelin,
The high-divers' amazing double spin.

We've done so well down on the river.
The cycle races made me shiver.
The heptathlon girls were in their stride
And beautiful London burst with pride.

The dressage with the lovely horses,
The sprinters rushing on their courses.
I thought the long jump was a lark
And football was played at St. James's Park.

We've welcomed people from many places
All wearing the colours of their races.
We've counted the medals with such great pride;
Gold, silver and bronze stood side by side.

But one gold medal makes me proud.
No National Anthem was sung out loud.
It was given to this man of mine
For forty-three years working down the mine!

Someday

Someday let me take you where
There's a place for us to share,
Down rainbow paths to silver streams,
Existing only in my dreams.

The crystal waters, cool and sweet,
With pearl-like pebbles at our feet.
Beyond the hills there's a leafy road
That leads us to our new abode.

Snow white sheep and happy herds,
Surrounded by your beloved birds.
A golden beach, a millpond sea,
Treasures there completely free.

Exotic blooms and emerald grass
Gently swaying as we pass.
Beloved faces of times long gone,
Outstretched arms to lead us on.

Worries and pain all left behind,
Happiness and joy are all we find.
On we go with clasping hands
Across the bridge to Paradise lands.

If Ever

If ever there should come a time
When I can't write another rhyme,
Unspoken words, I'll make amends,
To Sally, Nancy, Ena and all my friends.

When Doris, Lisa, Belle and John,
And Amy's childhood have all gone,
I hope my girls are happy wives,
And the boys do something with their lives.

I'm thankful for my happy life.
I hope I've been a decent wife.
I'm grateful for the love I've had.
For fun and laughter I'm so glad.

If I can't see John potter for hours,
Preparing the ground for next year's flowers;
When all life's debts have been wiped clean,
Lord, let me take my sewing machine!

Some Notes On 'Geordie'

For those of you unfamiliar with the peculiarities of Geordie 'language', the following may be helpful:

bairns are children

getting wrong off means *were told off by*

tight, as used to describe some of the men in the poems, does not mean tight-fisted or mean with money, but that they'd had a few too many drinks!

tret means *treated* – it is sometimes written as *treat,* but that gives the impression of a different pronunciation, so I have used the first spelling as that is how the word sounds if the poem is read out loud.

the town can be either Newcastle or Sunderland; Washington lies between them. Much is made in the media of the rivalry between the two larger towns (now actually both cities), especially when it comes to football, but what comes through in Lorna's poems is a sincere fondness for both.

Pensher is the correct spelling for the street called *Pensher View,* although the place is *Penshaw* and the famous monument which can be seen for miles is *Penshaw Monument.*

Parents are addressed as *mam* and *dad*. When talking about their parents, Geordies tend to say 'my' mam and 'my' dad, but they pronounce it 'me' – *me mam, me dad.*

mum is not generally used, as it is in other parts of the country, although Lorna has used it once in the poems, for rhyming purposes only!

Lorna and her sister Sally often addressed their mam as *mother.*

Grandparents are *grandma* and *grandad* or *granda* – *me grandma, me granda.* Some people say *nanna* for grandmother, but not in our family.

Children, grandchildren, brothers, sisters and cousins are addressed by name, but when we talk about them to other people, we use the pronoun *our* – *our Lorna, our Matty, our Norma, our Sally, our Joanne, our Mandy, our Kerry, our Ian, our Dawn, our Darren, our Alison, our Tony, our Gary.*

When talking about someone else's family, *our* is replaced by *your.*

These pronouns are meant to suggest a sense of belonging to a large, extended family, and tend not to be used in the south of England or even in some other parts of the north.

our Gyp (*Oxclose Dene*) was the family dog!

Geordie women of Lorna's generation and earlier rarely used the word 'husband'. Instead they used *man* – *my man, your man, her man* and some younger women still do so.

The word 'my' in this sense is pronounced 'my' (not 'me', as before), as it adds emphasis – he is *my* man (he belongs to *me!*)

American readers might like to know that *Washington Old Hall*, the ancestral home of the first president of the USA, still stands and is open to the public. One of its most prominent visitors was another president, Jimmy Carter, who planted a tree on the village green in a gesture of friendship as part of the bicentenary celebrations in the 1970s. He declared in Geordie: "Howay the lads!"

Alison Greaves

is the author of the following novels:

<u>The Inspector McClennan Murder Mysteries</u>
The Ayton Swans
The Secrets Of Seldom Seen
The Curse Of The Ayton Witches
A Cloak Of Pure White

<u>The 'Italy' Novels:</u>
Melanie's Face
In Vacanza

<u>and the dystopian thriller set in Newcastle-upon-Tyne:</u>
2022

contact Alison Greaves at: alisongreaves68@yahoo.com

Printed in Great Britain
by Amazon

43808495R00050